BLACK girl SHINE!

BEAUTIFUL

SMART

CONFIDENT

SELF LOVE

CHARACTER

Shavondra Walker
Ilustrated by AM Studio
Editor Renea Walker

Dedication

For the culture
Forever Yolanda & Alicia

Black girl, shine because you are Beautiful.

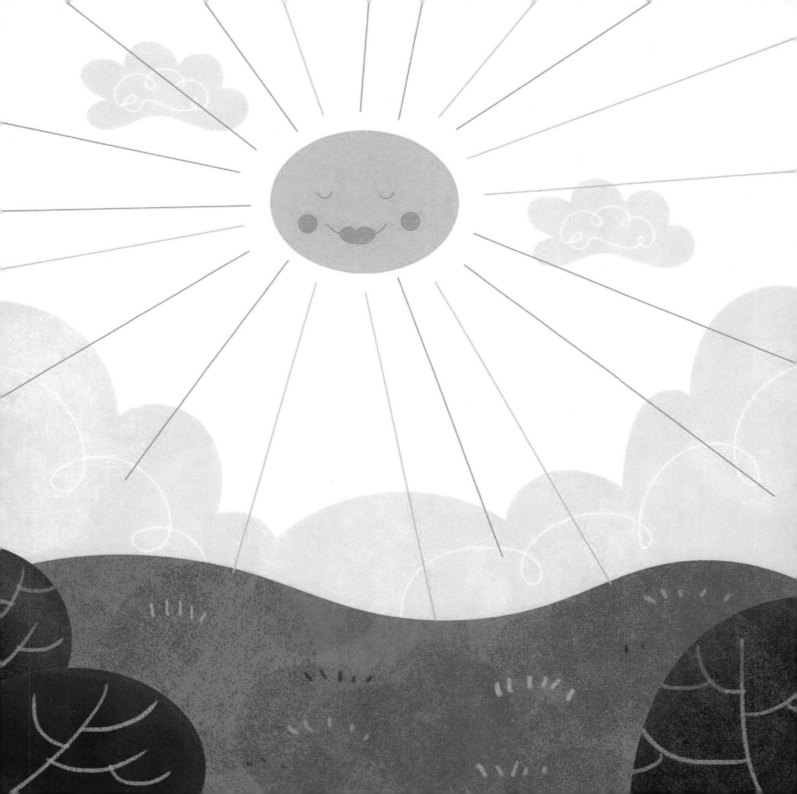

Your locs, kinky curls, and big afro are Beautiful you know!

Your brown skin, light skin, and dark skin is a sight to behold when the sun hits it; it shines like gold.

Round, slim, short, tall you are beautiful OVERALL!

Black girl, shine because you are Smart.

Fill your brain with books, you are more than good looks.

You can be a doctor and heal the sick.

You can be a lawyer and fight for human rights.

From businesswoman to ballerina you can accomplish anything.

Black girl, shine because you are Confident.

You are powerful!

You are magical!

Be confident in your ability to succeed.

You are a winner!

You have a voice!

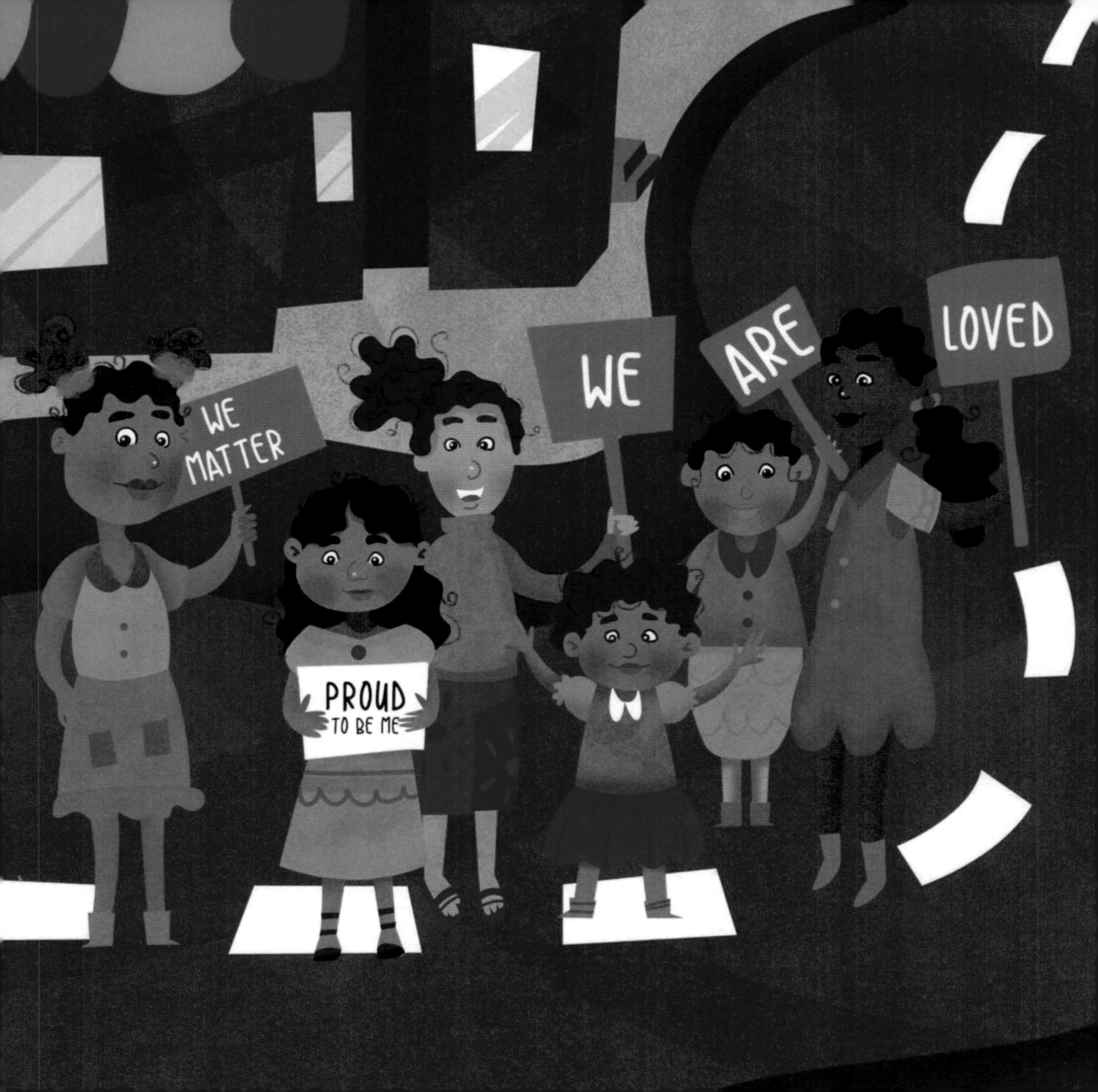
WE MATTER
PROUD TO BE ME
WE
ARE
LOVED

You are a leader!

Black girl, shine because of your Love for self.

I am royalty.

I wear the crown.

I matter,
and the world needs me.

My family loves and supports me.

I am blessed.

Black girl, shine because you have Character.

I am kind.

I am funny.

I am trustworthy.

I am honest and courageous.

I am respectful toward myself and others.

Black girl,
shine because you are...

Smart	Royal	Funny
Kind	Beautiful	Worthy
Loving	Confident	Loved
Respectful	Magical	Special

Thank You

I want to thank my family and friends for continuing to push me
beyond limitations and providing unlimited love and support.
I would also like to thank my editor for the hard work and long hours.
The Black Girl Shine team is phenomenal. I am forever grateful.